ISLAY AND JURA

Geese in flight and at rest, Loch Gorm

ISLAY AND JURA

GEORGE ROBERTSON

First published in Great Britain in 2006 by
Birlinn Ltd
West Newington House
10 Newington Road
Edinburgh EH9 1QS

www.birlinn.co.uk

ISBN10: 1 84158 428 2
ISBN13: 978 1 84158 428 7

British Library Cataloguing-in-Publication Data
A catalogue record for this book is available on request from the British Library

Printed and bound in Scotland

INTRODUCTION

SCOTLAND'S Inner Hebridean islands of Islay and Jura are special and unique to those who live there and to the thousands who visit every year. On the map of Scotland they point an angled fist down the side of the Kintyre peninsula towards Ireland. There they sit at the end of the Gulf Stream, occasionally kissed, but equally regularly over-flown, by the clouds of damp which fall on the west of the mainland. The islands tumble southwards from the whirlpool of Corrievreckan, via the landmark Paps of Jura and the twisting inlet of the 'other' Loch Tarbert, then across the turbulent, angry waters of the Sound of Islay to the green, grassy plains and beaches of Islay.

Round every corner you breathe history; the power and control of another age when command of the sea was the secret of dominating the land. In Islay's Finlaggan, Somerled – first Lord of the Isles, a title now held by the Price of Wales – used the might of the rowing galley to end the rule of the Vikings and went on to consolidate the hegemony of the Scots as far down as the Isle of Man. In Jura even earlier, they say that St Columba crossed the tiny land area in the centre of Jura to find his way north to settle in Iona.

Today, in contrast, peace is the hallmark of two islands of dramatic beauty and serenity. There are few signs of the warfare, the savagery and the turbulence of those distant days. In their place are communities of contented people and economies built on farming, fishing, tourism and the production of whisky.

It is the whisky of fine quality and unmistakable taste which has made these two islands as distinctive a region as Champagne and Burgundy in France and the Nappa Valley in California. Talk of Islay and people all too often think you say 'Ireland'. Say Jura and they think of a mountain region in France. But say Laphroaig or Lagavulin, Bowmore or Coal Ila, Ardbeg or Isle of Jura, Bruichladdich or Bunnahabhain, and suddenly geographic recognition dawns. The eight distilleries on two small islands create a trademark product, known, respected, admired, and enjoyed across the world.

To some it will seem unfair that, to the wider world, whisky defines the islands of Islay and Jura, despite their historical and natural richness. Yet in Rioja or Cognac, where natural beauty is also subordinate to the renowned alcohol of the region, people recognise the benefits, and capitalise on the fame of their region and its product. Likewise, the fact that whisky today brings so much enjoyment to so many who cannot even pronounce Islay is a matter for rejoicing.

These two islands are of course particularly special to me. I was born on Islay and my maternal grandfather, and his father too, were natives of the northern end of Jura. That makes me partial, but not blinkered. My roots are there; my formative years were spent in a near-idyllic environment which had space, freedom, no crime, and where the only threat to our youthful activities was our own carelessness in water and on rocks. It is, as a consequence, a very precious place to me, as it is to so many who know it.

We took our own children back to enjoy the magic and they in turn fell in love with it. The spell overcame even the lure of the discos and nightspots of adolescent-friendly resorts. The sea, the beaches and the scope for parent-free activity were a powerful attraction, and are now captivating yet another generation.

But these are special islands in objective and tangible ways as well; islands of long, fascinating history, of wild, complex geography and geology, of endlessly varied nature, of vivid and unforgettable scenery. They are islands of temperamental but temperate weather, with crystal clear light and the purest of air.

Although home in the nineteenth century to 14,000 people, and now to just over 3,000, an integrity has been preserved on the islands, and a way of life protected. There is a friendliness rare in many other island communities, and an openness and welcome that is warm and genuine to settler and visitor alike.

I felt immediately at home when I went to Iceland, to Barbados and to Bahrain in the Arabian Gulf. As different from Islay and Jura as they are, there is still no mistaking the island mentality, the immediate sense of self-containment. When your boundaries are defined by the sea, and your locality and neighbours as locked in as you are, in some ways you know your own limits and your own measure. The former Prime Minister of Iceland, David Oddson, told me of the visit there of Shimon Peres when he was Prime Minister of Israel. Peres surprised his hosts by saying that Iceland and Israel had much in common. 'First,' he said, 'we both got our independence in the 1940s. Second, our names start with the letter 'I'. And third, we are both surrounded by very hostile territory.'

'Ah!' said Oddson, 'We are different as well. You are the chosen people, but we are the frozen people.'

Iceland was also part of the empire of the Viking raiders of the Scottish coastline. The McDonalds, Lords of the Isles, drove out the Viking occupiers and for nearly two centuries (the thirteenth and fifteenth), dominated the whole west coast of Scotland. Reminders of Islay and Jura's history are the stuff of real-life legend: the ruins at Finlaggan, Dunyvaig Castle at Lagavulin, the stunningly beautiful and completely preserved ninth-century celtic cross at Kildalton and the fourteenth-/fifteenth-century one at Kilchoman.

Looking at Loch Finlaggan today, even with its progressing

excavations, the serenity belies the power which resided and was generated from there. The impact of plans, plots and politics radiated out from this modest little inland loch to the great sea-lochs and inlets, up glens and passes to the land mass of Scotland and right down to the Isle of Man.

Dunnyvaig Castle overlooks Lagavulin Bay, a naturally protected harbour where the galleys of the Lords were safe from attack, ready to go to sea and strike with remarkable force. Their naval commanders had simple ingenuity combined with the tenacity and toughness required to man the galleys, the warships of that time, without the GPS technology of today to point them in the right direction.

Both islands are steeped in history; small wonder since a glance at the map shows how strategically they were positioned. But that very location, on the main channel to mainland Britain, could spell tragedy as well as opportunity for mariners over the years. Islay's coasts in particular are surrounded by the sunken wrecks of those who perished through misadventure, miscalculation or the vagaries of wild Atlantic storms. The war graves at Kilchoman and Kilnaughton and the stark, sombre monument at the Mull of Oa give expression to the modern lives lost, though hundreds of others lie uncommemorated, victims of the will of nature.

The Oa Monument was erected by the US Red Cross after the end of the First World War to commemorate the American soldiers who died in the very last months of that war in the sinking of two troopships. The *Tuscania* was torpedoed off the Oa and the *Otranto* was sunk by collision at Machir Bay on the west coast. In all, 597 men died in these two American and British calamities. I know of both because my grandfather, Malcolm MacNeill, was at that time Police Sergeant at Bowmore and had the heavy responsibility for dealing with the disasters and the awesome aftermath.

Notwithstanding the tragedies of shipwrecks, including one still above the surface – the *Wyre Majestic* close to Bunnahabhain Distillery – the coasts of Islay and Jura are simply glorious. From the whirlpools of the Gulf of Corryvreckan in Jura's far north to the wild majesty of the Mull of Oa, there is every variety of scenery imaginable, including palm trees around Lochindaal.

Beaches like Saligo, Machir and Lossit on the west coast, washed by the mighty Atlantic Ocean, are simply spectacular. Gruinart's wide expanses and bijou Sanaigmore in the north, Kilnaughton and the 'Singing Sands' near Port Ellen and the seven-mile long beach called with commendable brevity and accuracy 'The Big Strand', offer a wide menu of dunes and seascape. Aside from sand, there is the wonder of Claggain Bay at the end of the Kildalton road. The raised beach there, with its almost scientifically graded and layered stones, holds enduring fascination for young and old alike.

Saligo Bay is, I confess, my and my family's favourite. Its waters are fatal for swimming, as quite a few foolhardy types have found, but the ever-changing and dramatic congruence of waves and rocks keeps the visitor spellbound. Children enjoy pools, caves, shelter and space. In addition, the light at Saligo is like nothing else I've ever known. Its quality and clarity are, quite simply, beyond description. The restless waves and tides, the rock formation which recalls Sydney's Opera House, the skies a limitless expanse with clouds the size of continents. The sand, shaped by the force of a billion tons of water, looks different every day. And out to sea, uninterrupted by any landfall, you will next touch dry land in Labrador. Saligo is a place of real beauty and enchantment and a photographer's paradise.

It is also a place without a mobile phone signal – another point in its favour. So it was to the amazement of all around one day when my cellphone rang. The caller was Michèle Aliot-Marie, the French Defence Minister. When she rang off, the phone, like all the others, again said 'No Signal'. The mystery remains as to how she alone penetrated Saligo's microwave barriers. Ah, those French.

Jura's beaches are less accessible than Islay's expanses. But the raised beaches of the roadless west coast are striking. You can see, as if it happened yesterday, the way in which the sea retreated, leaving the broad expanses of stones to be seen only by passing boats and seals. The one road on Jura, from its start at the Feolin Ferry, swiftly passes the wonders of Jura House and its exotic walled garden, and twists up the east coast. It links the tiny villages north of Craighouse, with its distillery, shop, hotel and surprising cluster of palm trees. It skirts Small Isles Bay and Lowlandman's Bay, passes Ardmenish, Lagg, Tarbet, where the island is almost severed by Loch Tarbert, and on up to Ardlussa. This northerly point is where my maternal great-grandfather, Hector MacNeill, was a shepherd. Despite the harshness of the life, he lived to the ripe old age of 83.

Indeed, many in Jura did live long and extraordinarily healthy lives. In the eighteenth century, the health of the inhabitants of Jura, TB apart, was considerably better than in any other part of the west of Scotland. Nobody has really identified a reason, but a new addition to the Jura population, a one-time US Army Intelligence Officer, Gary McKay, has pointed to a spring near Ardlussa which appears to have stimulant effects. It may be that this entirely natural energy drink could have had an impact no one ever imagined.

But Arlussa is not the last point on Jura. The road, and then a track, continue to Barnhill and beyond to Jura's own gulf. Barnhill is just a plain house standing on its own overlooking the sparse farmland down to the sea. What makes it important is not its architecture nor its lonely location but one particular inhabitant who called it home in the 1940s. Eric Blair, better known as George

Orwell, wrote with great force and fame. His masterpiece *1984* was written in Barnhill during the last few years of his life. The arduous existence Orwell imposed on himself here perhaps partly accounts for the bleak pessimism pervading the book.

Around that time, a stranger landed on my father's Police Station doorstep. He had missed the ferry and had nowhere to sleep. He requested, as some did in similar circumstances, a bed in the cells for the night. This was granted, and in the morning after eating my mother's porridge, he left. The signature 'E. Blair' meant nothing to my parents, but to the writing of the novel and to the description of the prisoner Winston's visit to the terrible 'Room 101', that night may have been decisive.

Today, Jura's population of 200 is dwarfed by its population of red deer. Once a wild species which provided sport for the island's wealthy landowners and their shooting parties, it is now farmed for its distinctive venison. But these are not normal farming methods – the deer freely wander the rugged open spaces of Jura and many a visiting walker or motorist has come face to face with a twelve-point stag.

Apart from the deer and some sheep, Jura has its own distillery with a new and proactive ownership and welcoming visitors' centre. Adverts featuring the map of Jura made from sheep's wool have given a whole new image to the softer spirit. There was once a time when the distilleries of Islay and Jura were secretive places discouraging visitors and casual callers with intimidating notices; but no longer.

It started with Bowmore, Islay's middle malt, and its pioneering visitors' centre. The Morrison family, and the former Distillery Manager Alistair Ross, discovered the value of local promotion and their visitors' centre became much more than a showcase for their popular whisky. Under the inimitable and high-octane leadership of Christine Logan, wave upon wave of visitors and industry guests gained a complete education in how whisky was made and why Islay whisky was the best.

Bowmore's impressive visitors' centre was to be followed by Jackie and Stewart Thomson's fine Kiln Café at Ardbeg, drawing visitors to the south east of the island. It has a restaurant, shop, exhibition and a collection of rare casks – one of which I 'filled' in 2000 and which is now silently and relentlessly maturing for the requisite ten to fifteen years.

Laphroaig Distillery, with its blazing white walls, more characteristic of a building on a Greek island, produces the most peaty of all malts. Across the road is a nondescript field which has been sold off by the square centimetre to foreigners wanting a piece of Islay. Not a few people have come up to me claiming, on the basis of this patch of rashes, to own a bit of 'my' island.

Then there is Lagavulin, the last of the three pearls on the east coast string. It too produces heavily peated whisky, an acquired taste like Laphroaig, and it sits on the shore of Somerled's 12th Century naval base. I remember visiting it when I represented the whisky workers' union and experiencing the dense atmosphere of the floor maltings, where germinating grain is stopped in its tracks in the first stage of the production of whisky. One of the men who laboured in this smoky cauldron complained that he and his compatriots deserved more money than the skilled stillmen who fine-tune the final stages of production. 'No more skill than a woman working a washing machine,' said the elderly maltman, unconcerned with the world of political correctness.

Bruichladdich is the born-from-the-dead distillery, revived by a group of local businessmen led by Sir John MacTaggart of Ardmore who brought in Managing Director Mark Ranier. The manager Jim McEwan, ex-Bowmore, is a true honey-voiced whisky believer who has just launched a Whisky Academy, bringing fascinated foreigners to 'The Laddie' to learn the secrets of the amber liquid.

Caol Ila for long kept its own counsel beside the Sound of Islay, its giant stills reflecting the water and the Paps of Jura. Its spirit was largely used for blending with other whiskies on the mainland but now, boasting its very own visitors' centre, it has become a connoisseur's choice as a rare and lighter Islay malt.

Bunnahabhain is the remotest distillery, at the end of a road winding past the inimitable Persabus Pottery with its green gloss celtic designs. This road has some of the most breathtaking views of Jura and eventually arrives at what is not just a distillery, but a village recalling a much more labour-intensive age. Bunnahabhain has also been scrubbed up too, and is near the pier where the small sea coasters called Puffers to take out the whisky casks before the age of bulk tankers.

As an Ileach myself I had some supreme advantages on Islay when I was union official for the Scotch Whisky industry. In these days I visited the island with my good friend and Rutherglen MP Gregor McKenzie, then Minister for Industry. We started our tour with Port Ellen Distillery, still working, and he sampled the local product. Gregor, always a keen fan of the golden liquid, savoured the generous measure and mused to the manager that with all this distilling expertise about there might be some private distilling going on. The Manager paused in that well-known Islay way and with a twinkle in the eye said, 'Why would they go to all that trouble and bother, when all they have to do is steal mine?'

During my time with NATO, thanks to Morrisons Bowmore, I gave their 17-year-old malt as my official gift to Presidents, Prime Ministers and Foreign and Defence Ministers. It was universally popular – even with those who did not drink the *usque beathe.*

The late President of Macedonia, Boris Trajkovski, when offered the Bowmore bottle with my personalised neck label, declared that he never drank alcohol because he was an 'orthodox Methodist'. Indeed he was, and a rarity among an Orthodox and Muslim population. When I sensed I may have committed a gaffe, I was about to withdraw the offending gift but he stopped me. 'But I thank you, because I have a lot of friends who are not orthodox Methodists'.

The President of Poland so loved the Bowmore that when he visited me in Brussels he took an unopened bottle of Ardbeg from my Islay malt collection, 'just to make a comparison'. The Foreign Minister of Spain's brother had a particular affection for my gift and the Supreme Allied Commander Europe had his aides scouring Brussels for a follow-up supply. So I did my bit to promote my island's most famous product.

When I chaired the NATO Summit in Prague in 2002, which was to invite seven new member states into membership of the Alliance, including three which only fifteen years before had been part of the Soviet Union, it was another chance to publicise Islay. Diageo, owners of Lagavulin, Coal Ila and the Port Ellen Maltings, gave me nineteen bottles of the remaining stock of Port Ellen. Since the distillery closed in 1983, bottles are becoming rarer and much sought after.

And so nineteen Presidents and Prime Ministers went home with a small part of that precious remaining stock and I convinced President George W. Bush, a vocal teetotaller in his recent years, to pose with the President of Latvia, Vaira Vike-Frieberga, as I presented the Czech President Vaclav Havel, one of my great heroes, with a specially boxed bottle of the product of my native village, Port Ellen.

Port Ellen is a tiny village surrounding a sparkling bay. It now has about 800 inhabitants and is one of the two island ferry ports. It has a lighthouse, as well it might, given the treacherous nature of the rocks in the vicinity, but one of unique square style,built in 1832 by Walter Frederick Campbell as a memorial to his wife Ellinor, after whom the village was named. It has the maltings, making the raw material for all the island's distilleries, a church – St Johns, where I was christened – and a super-active primary school, my own first tangle with education, with a charismatic Head Teacher, Violet Cusworth, and a well-merited reputation for innovation and community involvement.

But that's not all. Port Ellen has also produced a few interesting people in its time. Professor Sir Alistair Currie FRCP FRCPath, Professor of Pathology at Edinburgh University, was the son of the baker in Port Ellen and was President of the Royal Society of Edinburgh, Scotland's National Academy of Science and Letters, from 1991 to 1993, just before his premature death. He was followed as President later in the decade by Professor Sir William Stewart FRS, Professor of Biology at Dundee University and Government Chief Scientific Adviser to Prime Minister Margaret Thatcher. Bill, now Chairman of the nation's Health Protection Agency, was son of the janitor at Port Ellen Primary School.

A bit earlier, one Alexander McDougall was born at Portnatruin, just outside Port Ellen in 1732. Taken to New York by his father during the Clearances, he became a ship's captain, commanding two ships in the war with the French. He also prospered as a merchant, took up the cause of independence from Britain and was imprisoned for writing and distributing a 'seditious' pamphlet.

In the American War of Independence he headed the 1st New York Regiment and went on to serve as a Major General in George Washington's forces commanding the American troops at West Point. This was the key location on the River Hudson and is now the site of the US Military Academy. He was elected to the Continental Congress, the first in US history, and became America's first-ever Minister of the Marine. Before his early death in 1786, he was appointed founder President of the Bank of New York – the first Bank in the new United States of America.

Another Alexander McDougall, this time a sea captain who stayed with ships, is also said to have come from Port Ellen. He went to Canada where, in 1887, he invented a revolutionary cigar-shaped cargo ship for the Great Lakes called the Whaleback. The nineteen Whalebacks he built in Minnesota were for many years the most popular means of transporting goods around these great North American inland waterways.

Just up the road from Port Ellen is Kildalton, and the ruin of what was the once grand Kildalton Castle. This was the home of John Ramsay, from 1874 to 1886 Member of Parliament for the Falkirk Burghs constituency. This pre-universal suffrage constituency was a collection of Scottish Burghs including Linlithgow, Airdrie, Lanark and the town of Hamilton, which I was to represent a century later at Westminster for twenty-one years. Ramsay was one of the earliest business tycoons to invest in whisky and to take a modern approach to farming. Some say that he was a realist who recognised that overpopulation in the Oa and Kildalton was a recipe for social and economic disaster, so managed a planned emigration to Canada. Others say he was just another ruthless landowner who drove out the people in order to drive in the sheep. It is difficult to pass judgement, but those who went to Canada certainly prospered. Although he now lies in a grave buried in rhododendron bushes close to his castle, Ramsay lives on in the name of Port Ellen's village hall.

In more recent times, there has also been politics as well

as whisky in the Islay/Jura bloodstream. Major John Morrison MP – later Lord Margadale of Islay was laird of the Islay Estate, the biggest on the island. As Chairman of the 1922 Committee of all Conservative backbench MPs he was a hugely influential powerbroker. He famously hosted Margaret Thatcher in Islay House on her first summer holiday as Prime Minister in 1979. Apparently during her highly publicised stay she refused to wear Wellington boots on aesthetic grounds and hence destroyed a fair number of expensive shoes on muddy grounds. Lord Margadale had two sons in Parliament. Peter, a real character who served as Minister for Energy and was Mrs Thatcher's Parliamentary Private Secretary when she resigned and Charles, who never attained Ministerial office but as a liberal Tory attracted respect and affection. His daughter Mary eschewed politics for monarchy and is Lady-in-Waiting to the Queen.

Both John Smith, the late Labour Leader, and Brian Wilson, a recent Energy Minister, had parents living on Islay. Sir John McTaggart's sister, an Islay homeowner, is Fiona McTaggart MP for Slough and a former Home Office Minister; Alastair Carmichael, Liberal MP for Orkney and Shetland and a Gaelic speaker, is from the Oa; Tony Blair's father Leo was 'boarded out' in Bowmore during the war; Health Secretary Patricia Hewitt, herself from Australia, discovered recently she has Islay roots and David Cameron, the new Conservative Leader, regularly takes family holidays on Jura.

Islay has a golf course, although such a simple statement is wholly inadequate when it comes to the 'Machrie'. With its splendid hotel and chalets now owned by Graham Lacey and managed by Ian Brown, the Machrie Links golf course was designed by Willie Campbell in 1891. It is long, manicured and severely testing, with unusual and challenging hazards all of its own. Inspiring love and hate in equal measure, it swallows up golf balls in its impenetrable rough and experiences winds so strong that they carry your ball behind you if the angle is above twenty degrees. Sheep exercise their right to roam and wander unconcerned between golfers. Blind holes, and random contours mean that even the best golfers still play roulette at each tee. The views are distractingly inspirational and the weather changes at every hole.

Hundreds now pilgrimage each August from far and near for the famous Kildalton Cross competition. The trophy is a magnificent silver replica of the eighth-century Celtic cross. The original was stolen in one of Islay and Jura's very rare crimes and still remains lost, but all that adds to the lure of the competition.

In the Macedonia crisis of 2001, when the former Yugoslav state teetered on the brink of bloody civil war, I had a brief, much-interrupted break in Islay. It was a huge task to combine diplomatic and golf skills. Trying to speak on a mobile phone about tanks (misuse of), refugees (in escalating numbers), politicians and soldiers (from Chancellor Schroder to the Supreme Allied Commander) and contacts with violent insurgents (very secret), and all the while engaged with Machrie's bunkers or prone on the fairway writing a note, was neither simple nor good for the golf.

In the end the crisis was put right – but not the golf.

There is such variety on these two gentle, friendly isles. Round every corner, over every hill, in each village, there is something special and captivating: Portnahaven with its pioneering wave energy machine; Port Wemyss overlooking the Lighthouse on Orsay when the mist allows; Islay House, still majestic and now lovingly cared for by Tom Freidrich, which yearly hosts young musicians in concert; the square behind with a new range of small craft shops and Islay's own micro-brewery; Bridgend, Islay's crossing point with Campbell's modest shop hiding an Aladdin's cave of household goods; Craighouse, capital of Jura, with distillery, store and hotel squeezed together; by the river Sorn the Woollen Mill, still amazingly making its own cloth and now exporting to posh shops across the world; Kilchoman with its new mini-distillery at Rockfield Farm and The Ileach, a feisty and unmissable local paper edited by former hotelier Carl Reavey.

Ancient forts are prominent and undisturbed, lingering from a medieval age. Ruined hamlets still provide the evidence of those who hastily left for the new world. Cows cool themselves on the beach and in the water. Golden eagles and red-billed chuffs, the rarest of birds, and many thousands of commonest geese fill the sky. Temperamental seas are harvested for lobster, crab and delicious scallops.

From big names to big skies; from pristine beaches to famous distilleries; from solitude to quality hotels and fine food; from birdwatching and golfing to fishing, walking, sailing, riding or shooting; from dismal rain to brilliant sunshine: the variety of these two small islands is astounding. No wonder then that Islay and Jura are loved so much and visited by people who are drawn back again and again.

George Robertson

George Islay MacNeill Robertson (The Rt Hon Lord Robertson of Port Ellen KT GCMG honFRSE PC) was born in Port Ellen. He was MP for Hamilton and Hamilton South, Secretary of State for Defence and Secretary General of NATO. He is a keen amateur photographer whose pictures have been published widely. He regularly exhibits in the Parliamentary Photographic Exhibition and had his own exhibition in the Gallery of Modern Art, Tashkent, Uzbekistan.

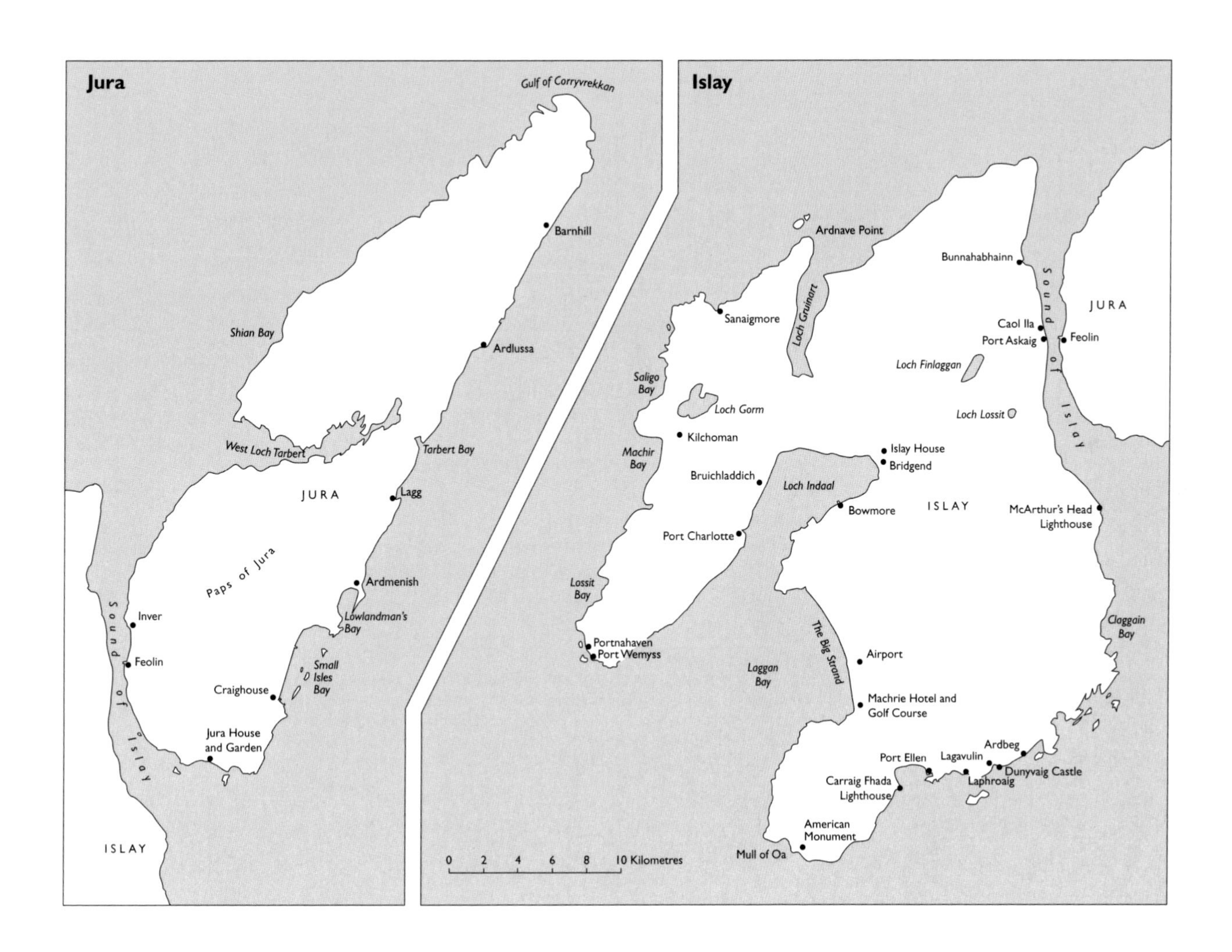
Jura
Gulf of Corryvrekkan
Barnhill
Ardlussa
Shian Bay
West Loch Tarbert
Tarbert Bay
JURA
Lagg
Paps of Jura
Ardmenish
Lowlandman's Bay
Sound of Islay
Inver
Feolin
Small Isles Bay
Craighouse
Jura House and Garden
ISLAY
Islay
Ardnave Point
Bunnahabhainn
Sanaigmore
Loch Gruinart
Sound of Islay
JURA
Caol Ila
Port Askaig
Feolin
Loch Finlaggan
Saligo Bay
Loch Gorm
Loch Lossit
Kilchoman
Machir Bay
Islay House
Bridgend
Bruichladdich
Loch Indaal
Bowmore
ISLAY
McArthur's Head Lighthouse
Port Charlotte
Lossit Bay
Claggain Bay
Portnahaven
Port Wemyss
The Big Strand
Airport
Laggan Bay
Machrie Hotel and Golf Course
Ardbeg
Port Ellen
Lagavulin
Dunyvaig Castle
Carraig Fhada Lighthouse
Laphroaig
American Monument
Mull of Oa
0 2 4 6 8 10 Kilometres

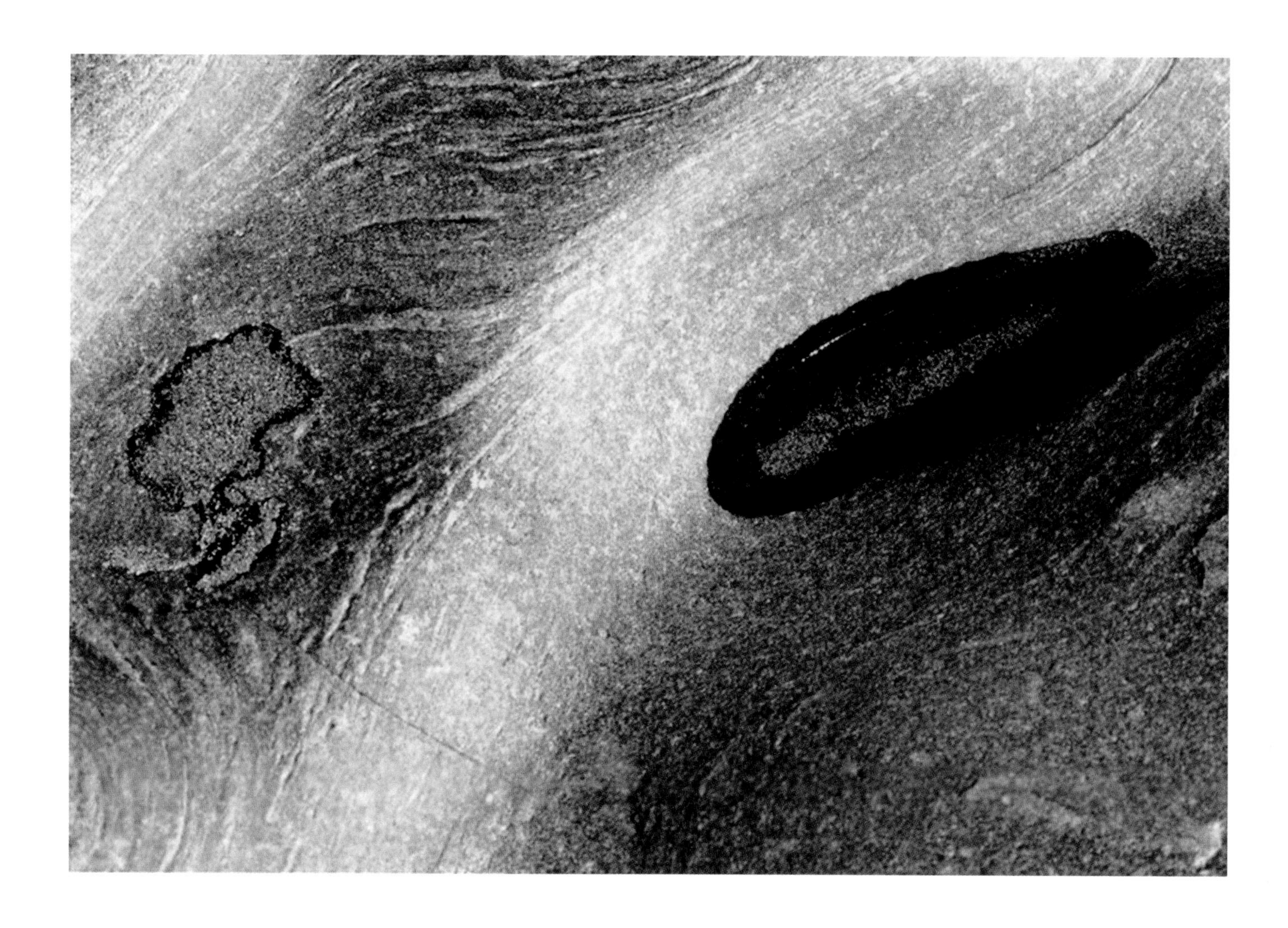

Sand, water and rock

View from Caol Ila Distillery, Sound of Islay

Graham and Isabelle Allison, proprietors, Port Charlotte Hotel

Medieval Fort, a farm on Islay

Steve Martin, storekeeper, Craighouse, Jura

Entrance to Walled Garden, Jura House

Paps in the mist

Peace and tranquillity, Loch Gruinart, Islay

Port Ellen Distillery, closed 1983

Loch Gruinart

Storm at Saligo Bay

Port Ellen Bay

Low sun at West Loch Tarbert, Jura

Rachael scores on Saligo sand

Shells on driftwood, Saligo

Celtic Cross at the derelict church at Kilchoan

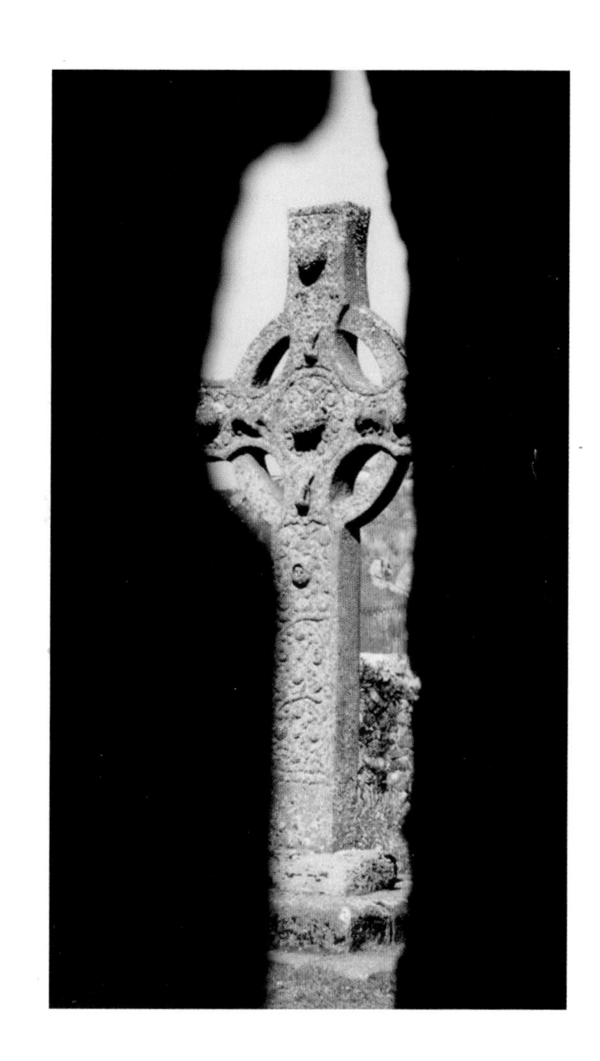

The Kildalton Cross

The landscape above Lagavulin

Lagavulin Distillery

The Port Ellen Lighthouse, Carraig Fhada, Islay

McArthur's Head Lighthouse

Rollers at Lossit Bay, by Portnahaven

Geese returning to Loch Indaal at dusk

Cattle on the beach, Lossit Bay

Flowers on the cliff face

Peats drying

Jura milestone

Postbox at Laphroaig Distillery

Loch Gruinart through the window of Kilchiaran Church

Dawn on the Low Road

Ferry at Port Ellen Pier

Fuschia bush, a Jura speciality

Remains of the headquarters of the Lords of the Isles, Loch Finlaggan, Islay

Sunset over Loch Indaal

The MV *Isle of Arran* evening sailing to Port Ellen

Bruno Schroder of Dunlossit Estate (testing kerosene, not whisky!)

Islay Pipe Band

Debris of the fishing

Dawn at Port Ellen

Ardbeg Pagodas

Caol Ila casks

Ardlussa Bay

The Head of Loch Tarbert, Jura

Isla Swanson, Bowmore Bakery

Remembering John Ramsay, Ramsay Hall, Port Ellen

Katie McIndeor, barmaid, Bridgend Hotel

Port Ellen with the Police Station overlooking the bay

Pat Roy, the Celtic House, Bowmore

Croft at Newton, Islay

Liz Sykes, batik artist, Islay House Square

Oystercatchers on the Big Strand

Christine Logan, long-time manager of the Visitor Centre, Bowmore Distillery

The Islay Lifeboat, *Helmut Schroder,* Port Askaig

The Main Drag, Craighouse, Jura

Jura Parish Church

In flight over Loch Indaal

Surprised deer

Lowlandsman's Bay, Jura

Loerin Farm, near Port Ellen, Islay

Rock falls on the Sound of Islay

Remains of a chimney stack, abandoned village

Gravestones of the crew of HMS *Otranto*, Kilchoan

Reflections of a blue cask

Dunyvaig Castle, Lagavulin, Islay

The Round Church, Bowmore

Craighouse, Jura

Craighouse in the shadows

A dog passed here, Saligo

The Sydney Opera House rocks beyond Smaull

Clouds on the Paps

Stones of Destiny, Claggain Bay

Ardbeg Distillery

Between storms at Saligo

Bowmore Distillery

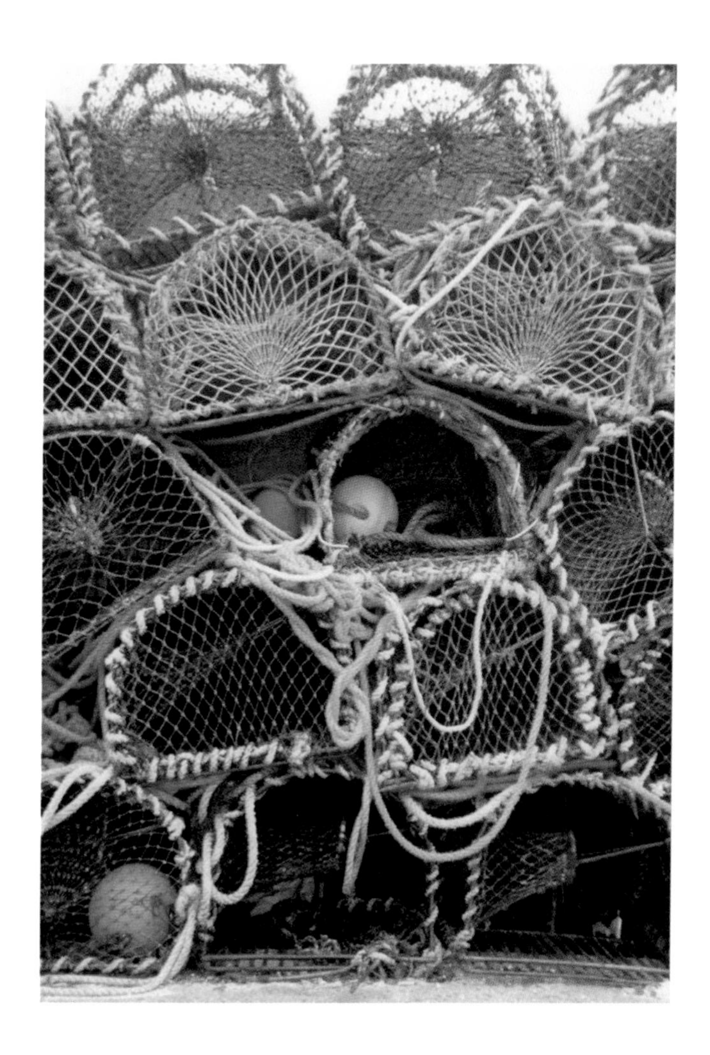

Creels at Bowmore Pier

Birds at rest

Bowmore skyline

Snow on the Paps of Jura

Joan Brown with prize highland cow at the Islay, Jura and Colonsay Agricultural Annual Show 2005, Gruinart

Show prizes and uninterested visitor

Bowmore's Round Church

Birds on the wing

Birthday fireworks at Loch Lossit

Enthusiasm in a Bruichladdich still

Bruichladdich Distillery

St Kieran's Church, Port Charlotte

Port Charlotte Lighthouse

Main Street, Port Charlotte

Waiting for summer, Port Charlotte

Mull of Oa and the American Monument from Port Charlotte

Blackface Tup

Captain Tom Friedrich, ex-US Navy Vietnam pilot and aeronautic specialist, and owner and custodian of Islay House, with his granddaughter, Stella

Loch Gorm and surrounding moss

Ninth green, the Machrie Golf Course

Claggian Bay

Port Charlotte from the sea

Small Isles Bay, Jura

Beach at Machir Bay

Wreck of the MV *Wyre Majestic* overlooked by the Paps of Jura

The American Monument, Mull of Oa, Islay

Lagg. Jura

Raised beach on the west coast of Jura

Jack Paton, Jura's oldest resident, Craighouse,

Portnahaven reflection

Violet Cusworth, Headteacher, Port Ellen Primary School

Lily 'Fish' McDougall – piper, artist, hunter, storyteller – in her ninth decade, Yellow Rock Cottage, Coal Ila

Odd angles at Port Wemyss and the Orsay Lighthouse

Jackie and Emma at Ardbeg's Kiln Café

Cruach Croft at sunset

Sally Christie, Mary McKenzie and Alison McLellan, The Islay Whisky Shop

Crossroads at the Oa

Sunset at Machir Bay